Master Your Writing: A Comprehensive Guide to Correcting Common Grammar Mistakes

Created by: Marvelous O.

Disclaimer

The information provided in this book is intended for educational and informational purposes only. The author, Marvelous O., has made every effort to ensure that the content presented in this book is accurate, complete, and up-to-date. However, the author and publisher do not guarantee the accuracy, completeness, or usefulness of the information contained herein, and accept no liability for any errors or omissions that may be present.

The reader assumes full responsibility for using the information contained in this book. The author and publisher disclaim any liability or responsibility for any loss or damage that may be incurred as a result of using the information presented in this book. The information provided in this book is not a substitute for professional advice, and readers are advised to seek the guidance of qualified professionals in specific situations.

The author and publisher do not endorse or recommend any particular product or service mentioned in this book. Any opinions expressed in this book are solely those of the author and do not necessarily reflect the views of the publisher.

This book is protected under international copyright laws and treaties. No part of this book may be reproduced or transmitted in any form or by any means, electronic or mechanical, including photocopying, recording, or by any information storage and retrieval system, without permission in writing from the publisher.

By reading and using the information contained in this book, you acknowledge and agree to the terms and conditions outlined in this disclaimer.

Introduction

In today's fast-paced and ever-evolving world, communication has become an essential part of our daily lives. From business emails to social media posts, the way we express ourselves matters more than ever. However, with the rise of instant messaging and text-speak, the art of grammar and punctuation seems to have taken a back seat. As a result, it's becoming increasingly common to see people making errors in their writing and speaking, whether it's in their personal or professional lives.

This new book is designed to help people identify and correct the most common grammar errors that occur in both spoken and written communication. It is aimed at anyone who wants to improve their language skills, from students and young professionals to seasoned writers and educators.

The book covers a wide range of topics, including punctuation, verb tenses, subject-verb agreement, pronouns, and sentence structure. Each chapter is dedicated to a specific topic, and the information is presented in a clear and concise manner, making it easy to understand and apply in real-world situations.

The book also includes practical exercises and quizzes to help readers practice what they have learned, ensuring that they can apply the information to their own writing and speaking. The quizzes are designed to be interactive, allowing readers to test their knowledge and receive instant feedback on their performance.

In addition, the book features examples of common grammar errors, and provides explanations and corrections for each. This helps readers to understand the context in which the error occurs, and how to avoid making the same mistake in the future.

Whether you're a student struggling with academic writing, a professional looking to improve your business communication, or simply someone who wants to brush up on their language skills, this book is an invaluable resource. It provides a comprehensive guide to the most common grammar errors, and offers practical advice and exercises to help readers improve their communication skills.

Importance Of Proper Grammar

Proper grammar is essential in communication. It helps to ensure that the message being conveyed is clear and easily understood by the intended audience. The use of correct grammar helps to avoid ambiguity, misunderstandings, and confusion, which can result in miscommunication and errors. Proper grammar also adds credibility to the speaker or writer and enhances the overall quality of the message.

One of the primary reasons why proper grammar is crucial is that it helps to maintain a professional image. Whether you are writing a job application, presenting a business proposal, or simply communicating with your colleagues, using proper grammar demonstrates your attention to detail and your commitment to professionalism. It also helps to establish trust and confidence in your abilities.

In addition to maintaining a professional image, proper grammar is also essential for academic success. In academia, the quality of your writing is often judged by the grammar and language you use. Professors and instructors expect their students to use proper grammar, and those who fail to do so may be penalized with lower grades. Proper grammar also plays a vital role in research papers, essays, and other written assignments, as it helps to convey complex ideas and arguments in a clear and concise manner.

Proper grammar is also critical in the workplace. In many professions, written communication is a crucial part of daily tasks, including emails, memos, reports, and other types of documents. Poor grammar in these types of documents can damage the reputation of the company, undermine the authority of the writer, and result in costly errors.

Beyond professional and academic settings, proper grammar is essential for personal communication as well. Good grammar helps to ensure that your messages are interpreted correctly by your friends, family, and other acquaintances. It also helps to convey respect and consideration for the recipient of the message, which can strengthen relationships and foster a sense of community.

Finally, proper grammar is an essential skill that can benefit individuals throughout their lives. It can help with the development of critical thinking and analytical skills, as well as improve overall communication abilities. By developing strong grammar skills, individuals can communicate more effectively and confidently in all aspects of their lives, leading to greater success and personal satisfaction.

Common Grammar Errors

Common grammar errors are mistakes made in the use of language that violate accepted rules of grammar. They can range from simple spelling mistakes to more complex errors in sentence structure, verb tense, subject-verb agreement, punctuation, and more. These errors can occur in both spoken and written communication and can lead to misunderstandings or confusion for the reader or listener. Some of the most common grammar errors include confusing homophones (words that sound the same but have different meanings and spellings), using incorrect verb forms, and incorrect punctuation usage. Identifying and correcting common grammar errors is an essential skill for effective communication in any context, including academic, professional, and personal communication. Subject-verb agreement is a common grammar error that occurs when the subject and verb in a sentence do not agree in number. For example, "The boy is playing" instead of "The boys are playing."

Here are more examples of the common Grammars;

1. Misplaced modifiers occur when a modifier is placed too far away from the word or phrase it is intended to modify, leading to confusion or ambiguity. For example, "I saw a car driving on the road with a broken windshield" instead of "I saw a car with a broken windshield driving on the road."

2. Using the wrong verb tense is a common error that can make writing confusing or unclear. For example, "I will go to the store yesterday" instead of "I went to the store yesterday."

3. Confusing homophones is another common error, where words that sound the same but have

different meanings are used interchangeably. For example, "their" and "there," or "your" and "you're."

4. Incorrect punctuation is a common grammar error, including the misuse of commas, apostrophes, and quotation marks. For example, "He said, 'I'll be back tomorrow', and left" instead of "He said, 'I'll be back tomorrow,' and left."

5. Using the wrong word order can also lead to errors in grammar, such as placing adverbs in the wrong position in a sentence. For example, "I only eat pizza on Fridays" instead of "I eat pizza only on Fridays."

6. Capitalization errors are common, including the incorrect capitalization of proper nouns or the overuse of capital letters in a sentence. For example, "The president of the United States was Born in hawaii" instead of "The President of the United States was born in Hawaii."

7. Using double negatives can also lead to confusion and is considered a grammatical error. For example, "I don't want no more candy" instead of "I don't want any more candy."

8. Misusing prepositions is another common grammar error, such as using "of" instead of "from" or "with" instead of "in." For example, "I live of California" instead of "I live in California."

9. Confusing singular and plural nouns is another common error that can cause confusion or ambiguity. For example, "The data is incorrect" instead of "The data are incorrect."

10. Using the wrong pronoun case, such as "me" instead of "I" or "who" instead of "whom," is also considered a common grammar error. For example, "Him and me went to the store" instead of "He and I went to the store."

11. Incorrectly using possessive apostrophes, such as "it's" instead of "its," is another common grammar error. For example, "The dog wagged it's tail" instead of "The dog wagged its tail."

12. Failing to use articles correctly, such as "a" or "an," is another common error that can make writing confusing or unclear. For example, "I saw cat in park" instead of "I saw a cat in the park."

13. Using incomplete or run-on sentences is another common grammar error, such as "She went to the store, she bought some milk" instead of "She went to the store and bought some milk."

14. Confusing irregular verbs can also lead to grammatical errors, such as using "teached" instead of "taught" or "runned" instead of "ran."

15. Using passive voice instead of active voice can also lead to unclear or awkward sentences. For example, "The ball was hit by the boy" instead of "The boy hit the ball."

Chapter One
<u>Subject-Verb Agreement</u>

Subject-verb agreement is a fundamental concept in English grammar that refers to the relationship between the subject of a sentence and the verb that follows it. The basic rule of subject-verb agreement is that a singular subject takes a singular verb, while a plural subject takes a plural verb. For example, "He runs" is correct, while "He run" is incorrect because the subject "he" is singular and requires the singular verb "runs".

However, there are many exceptions and complexities to the basic rule of subject-verb agreement that can make it challenging to master. One of the most common exceptions is with subjects that are collective nouns, which can be either singular or plural depending on the context. For example, "The team is practicing" is correct because "team" is considered a singular entity, while "The team are arguing" is also correct because the emphasis is on the individual members of the team and not the team as a singular entity.

Another exception to the basic rule is with subjects that are composed of two or more nouns connected by "and". If both nouns are singular, they take a plural verb, while if one of the nouns is plural, the verb should be singular. For example, "The cat and the dog are sleeping" is correct because both nouns are singular, while "The cat and the dogs are sleeping" is incorrect because one of the nouns is plural.

Other exceptions to subject-verb agreement include irregular verbs, where the past tense does not end in "-ed", and indefinite pronouns, such as "anyone" and "everyone", which are always singular.

To ensure correct subject-verb agreement, it is essential to identify the subject of a sentence and determine whether it is singular or plural before choosing the appropriate verb form. It is also important to be aware of the many exceptions and complexities that can arise in subject-verb agreement, and to consult a reliable grammar guide or language expert when in doubt.

In conclusion, subject-verb agreement is a critical aspect of English grammar that plays a vital role in clear and effective communication. By understanding the basic rule of subject-verb agreement and the many exceptions and complexities that can arise, writers and speakers can avoid common errors and ensure that their messages are conveyed accurately and clearly.

<u>Definition And Series Of Its Examples</u>

Subject-verb agreement is also a concept in grammar that refers to the way in which the subject and verb in a sentence must agree in terms of their number and person. Failure to adhere to this rule can result in awkward or confusing sentences that are difficult to read and understand.

For more example, consider the following sentence: "The dog barks loudly." In this sentence, the subject ("the dog") is singular, and the verb ("barks") is also singular. This agreement between subject and verb ensures that the sentence is clear and easy to understand.

Now, let's consider a sentence that violates subject-verb agreement: "The dogs barks loudly." Here, the subject ("the dogs") is plural, but the verb ("barks") is singular. This error creates confusion for the reader and makes the sentence grammatically incorrect. The correct sentence would be "The dogs bark loudly," where the plural subject is paired with the plural verb "bark."

Another example of subject-verb agreement can be seen in the sentence "She runs every morning." Here, the subject ("she") is singular, and the verb ("runs") is also singular. On the other hand, consider the sentence "They run every morning." Here, the subject ("they") is plural, and the verb ("run") is also plural, reflecting the agreement between the subject and verb.

Subject-verb agreement can become more complex when dealing with compound subjects, indefinite pronouns, and collective nouns. Compound subjects refer to two or more subjects joined by a conjunction, such as "and" or "or." In these cases, the verb should agree with the number of the closest subject. For example, "The cat and the dog sleep on the bed" requires the plural verb "sleep" because the closest subject, "dog," is plural.

Indefinite pronouns, such as "everyone" or "somebody," can also present challenges for subject-verb agreement. These pronouns can be either singular or plural, depending on the context. For instance, "Everyone knows the answer" requires a singular verb because the indefinite pronoun is singular, while "Somebody left their book on the table" requires a plural verb because "somebody" refers to an unknown number of people.

Finally, collective nouns, such as "team" or "family," can take either singular or plural verbs depending on how they are used. For example, "The team is playing well" requires the singular verb "is" because the team is being treated as a single unit, while "The team are arguing among themselves" requires the plural verb "are" because the members of the team are being treated as individuals.

In summary, subject-verb agreement is an important concept in grammar that requires the subject and verb in a sentence to agree in terms of their number and person. Correct subject-verb agreement can help to ensure clear and effective communication, while errors can create confusion and make sentences difficult to read and understand. By understanding the basic rules of subject-verb agreement, writers and speakers can improve their communication skills and avoid common grammatical errors.

Common Mistakes And How To Avoid Them

Here are ten common mistakes and how to avoid them:

1. **Incomplete subjects -** Sometimes the subject of a sentence can be omitted, making it difficult to determine the appropriate verb to use. To avoid this mistake, ensure that every sentence has a clear and complete subject that agrees with the verb.

2. Compound subjects - When a sentence has a compound subject (i.e., two or more subjects connected by "and"), the verb should be plural. For example, "John and Mary are going to the park."

3. Collective nouns - Collective nouns such as team, family, and group are singular and require a singular verb. For example, "The team is playing well."

4. Indefinite pronouns - Indefinite pronouns such as everyone, someone, anyone, and nobody are singular and require a singular verb. For example, "Everyone is here."

5. Singular and plural nouns - When a singular noun is connected to a plural noun with "or" or "nor," the verb agrees with the noun closest to it. For example, "The cat or the dogs are outside."

6. Intervening phrases - When there is an intervening phrase between the subject and verb, it is easy to use the wrong verb form. To avoid this mistake, always identify the subject before selecting the verb.

7. Titles and names - When a title or name is used as a subject, it is treated as singular and requires a singular verb. For example, "The President is delivering a speech."

8. Time and distance - When time and distance are used as subjects, they are considered singular and require a singular verb. For example, "Five miles is a long distance to walk."

9. Quantities - When a quantity is used as a subject, the verb agrees with the noun that follows it. For example, "Ten dollars was all he had."

10. Subject-verb agreement in questions - In questions, the subject and verb are inverted, but they still need to agree in number. For example, "Are the boys playing soccer?"

Practice Exercises

Exercise 1:

Write the correct verb form in parentheses for each sentence.

1. My friends (is/are) coming over for dinner tonight.
2. The book on the shelf (belongs/belong) to me.
3. Neither the cats nor the dog (likes/like) to be left alone.
4. The sound of the waves (calms/calm) me down.
5. The group of students (was/were) excited to go on the field trip.

Exercise 2:

Identify the subject and verb in each sentence and determine if they agree in number. If they don't, correct the sentence.

1. The cat on the windowsill is meowing loudly.
2. The students in the classroom is taking a test.
3. My mom and dad loves to travel.
4. The pile of books on the desk need to be organized.
5. Each of the students were given a different assignment.

Exercise 3:

Rewrite each sentence using the correct subject-verb agreement.

1. There is many reasons why I want to travel the world.
2. The group of tourists was admiring the view of the city from the top of the hill.
3. The collection of stamps are worth a lot of money.

4. The athlete, along with his coach, have been training hard for the competition.
5. The news about the storm are spreading quickly.

Chapter Two
Pronoun Usage

Pronouns are a crucial part of English grammar, allowing speakers and writers to avoid repetitive use of nouns and to refer to individuals or objects with greater ease. However, incorrect or inconsistent use of pronouns can lead to confusion, ambiguity, and even unintentional offense. To avoid these issues, it is important to understand the different types of pronouns and how they should be used in different contexts.

Personal pronouns are perhaps the most commonly used type of pronoun, and they refer to individuals or groups of people. These pronouns include "I," "you," "he," "she," "it," "we," and "they." Personal pronouns should be used consistently throughout a sentence or paragraph to avoid confusion. For example, using "he" to refer to a person in one sentence and "they" in the next can be unclear and confusing for readers.

Relative pronouns are used to introduce a subordinate clause and to connect it to an independent clause. Common relative pronouns include "who," "whom," "whose," "which," and "that." It is important to use the correct relative pronoun based on whether the subject is a person or a thing, and whether it is the subject or object of the sentence.

Reflexive pronouns are used to refer to the subject of a sentence when the subject is also the object of the sentence. For example, "I washed myself" or "She gave herself a pat on the back." It is important to use reflexive pronouns correctly and avoid using them unnecessarily, as they can sound awkward or redundant.

Demonstrative pronouns are used to point out or identify specific people, places, or things. Common demonstrative pronouns include "this," "that," "these," and "those." It is important to use demonstrative pronouns consistently and accurately to avoid confusion and ambiguity.

Indefinite pronouns refer to individuals or objects in a non-specific or general way. Examples of indefinite pronouns include "everyone," "someone," "nothing," and "anything." Indefinite pronouns can be tricky to use correctly, as their meaning can be affected by the context of the sentence.

Finally, possessive pronouns are used to show ownership or possession of a person, place, or thing. Examples of possessive pronouns include "mine," "yours," "his," "hers," "ours," and "theirs." It is important to use possessive pronouns correctly to avoid confusion and to show ownership or possession clearly.

Pronoun usage is a fundamental aspect of English grammar that can greatly affect the clarity and coherence of written and spoken communication. By understanding the different types of pronouns and how they should be used in different contexts, speakers and writers can avoid confusion, ambiguity, and unintentional offense, and create more effective and persuasive messages.

Definition And Examples Of Pronoun

A pronoun is a word that is used in place of a noun or a noun phrase. They can be used to replace the noun, or they can be used to refer to it indirectly. Pronouns are a part of speech that helps speakers and writers avoid the repetitive use of nouns in their sentences.

Here are ten examples of pronouns:

1. **Personal Pronouns:** They are used to refer to specific people or things. Examples include I, you, he, she, it, we, and they. For instance: "She gave him the book she was reading."

2. **Possessive Pronouns:** They show ownership or possession of a noun. Examples include mine, yours, his, hers, its, ours, and theirs. For example: "The book is mine."

3. **Demonstrative Pronouns**: They point to or indicate specific nouns. Examples include this, that, these, and those. For example: "That is my car."

4. **Reflexive Pronouns**: They refer back to the subject of a sentence. Examples include myself, yourself, himself, herself, itself, ourselves, and themselves. For example: "I hurt myself."

5. **Relative Pronouns:** They are used to connect two clauses in a sentence. Examples include who, whom, whose, that, and which. For example: "The book that I read was interesting."

6. **Interrogative Pronouns**: They are used to ask questions. Examples include who, whom, whose, what, which, and where. For example: "Who is coming to the party?"

7. **Indefinite Pronouns:** They are used to refer to non-specific people or things. Examples include anyone, everyone, no one, someone, anybody, and nobody. For example: "Everybody is welcome."

8. **Distributive Pronouns:** They are used to refer to individual items in a group. Examples include each, either, and neither. For example: "Either of the books is fine."

9. **Reciprocal Pronouns:** They are used to indicate a mutual action or relationship. Examples

include each other and one another. For example: "They love each other."

10. **Emphatic Pronouns:** They are used to add emphasis to a noun or pronoun. Examples include himself, herself, and themselves. For example: "He himself cleaned the room."

Pronouns are a vital part of language, and they help us to avoid repeating the same noun over and over again in our sentences. There are many types of pronouns, including personal pronouns, possessive pronouns, demonstrative pronouns, reflexive pronouns, relative pronouns, interrogative pronouns, indefinite pronouns, distributive pronouns, reciprocal pronouns, and emphatic pronouns. By using the correct pronouns, we can make our writing and speech more concise and clear, and ensure that our message is communicated effectively.

Common Mistake And How To Avoid Them

Pronouns are an essential part of language that replaces nouns to prevent repetition and make communication smoother. However, using pronouns can be tricky, and mistakes can often occur. Common mistakes in pronoun usage include errors in gender, number, case, and agreement. In this article, we will discuss some of these errors and provide tips on how to avoid them.

1. **Confusing Gender**: One common mistake in pronoun usage is confusing gender. In English, there are gender-specific pronouns such as "he" and "she," and gender-neutral pronouns such as "they" and "them." When referring to a person, it is essential to use the correct gender pronoun. Using the wrong pronoun can be offensive and disrespectful. A tip to avoid this error is to ask the person for their preferred pronoun.

2. **Singular or Plural:** Another common mistake in pronoun usage is using the wrong number. In English, there are singular and plural pronouns such as "he" and "they." It is important to use the correct pronoun according to the number of the noun it replaces. For example, "she" is singular, and "they" is plural. An easy way to avoid this mistake is to make sure the pronoun matches the number of the noun.

3. **Case Errors**: Pronouns can also be in different cases, such as subjective, objective, and possessive. Common mistakes in case usage include using the wrong case or mixing different cases in the same sentence. For example, "me and him went to the store" should be "he and I went to the store." A tip to avoid case errors is to pay attention to the role of the pronoun in the sentence and choose the correct case accordingly.

4. **Antecedent Agreement:** Another common mistake in pronoun usage is antecedent

agreement. The antecedent is the noun that the pronoun replaces. Pronouns must agree with their antecedents in number and gender. For example, "Each student must bring their book" should be "Each student must bring his or her book." An easy way to avoid this mistake is to use gender-neutral language or rephrase the sentence to avoid using a pronoun.

5. **Vague Pronoun Reference:** Using vague pronoun reference is another common mistake in pronoun usage. This occurs when it is unclear which noun the pronoun refers to. For example, "John told Bill that he would come" could mean either John or Bill would come. A tip to avoid this mistake is to make sure the pronoun has a clear antecedent, or rephrase the sentence to avoid using a pronoun.

6. **Reflexive Pronouns:** Reflexive pronouns such as "myself" and "yourself" are often misused in sentences. Common mistakes include using them incorrectly or unnecessarily. For example, "She gave the present to myself" should be "She gave the present to me." An easy way to avoid this mistake is to use reflexive pronouns only when they are necessary and to use the correct form.

7. **Pronoun Order:** Pronoun order is another common mistake in pronoun usage. In English, the order of pronouns is subject, object, and possessive. For example, "He and me went to the store" should be "He and I went to the store." A tip to avoid this mistake is to remember the correct order and make sure the pronouns are in the correct form.

8. **Pronoun Agreement with Collective Nouns**: Pronoun agreement is an essential aspect of English grammar, and a common mistake in this area is with collective nouns. A collective noun refers to a group of people or things, such as "team," "family," or "committee." The mistake often made is to use a singular pronoun to refer to a collective noun, which is technically incorrect. The correct usage is to use a plural pronoun to match the collective noun's plural form. For example, instead of saying, "The team did their best, but they lost the game," one might incorrectly say, "The team did its best, but it lost the game." The latter sentence is incorrect because the team is made up of multiple individuals, so the pronoun "its" should be replaced with the plural pronoun "their."

9. Another common pronoun mistake is the misuse of **personal pronouns**. For instance, confusing "me" and "I" or "she" and "her" in a sentence is a common error. One way to avoid this mistake is by testing the sentence without the other subject. For example, "She and I went to the store" could be tested by taking out the "she" portion, leaving just "I went to the store." Similarly, "Give the book to her and me" could be tested as "Give the book to

me" to ensure that the correct pronoun is used. Additionally, it is important to remember that "who" is used as a subject, and "whom" is used as an object, so one might say "Who is going to the party?" instead of "Whom is going to the party?" to avoid this common mistake. By paying close attention to pronoun agreement and usage, one can improve their English grammar and avoid these common errors

Practice Exercises

Exercise 1: Pronoun Agreement

In the following sentences, identify the incorrect pronoun agreement and rewrite the sentence using the correct pronoun.

1. The committee announced their decision.
2. Each of the students brought their own lunch.
3. Neither of the dogs wagged its tail.

Exercise 2: Vague Pronoun Reference

In the following sentences, identify the pronoun with a vague or unclear antecedent and rewrite the sentence to clarify the reference.

1. The teacher gave the students an assignment, but they didn't understand it.
2. Emily and her sister went to the mall, but she forgot her purse.
3. The CEO addressed the employees, but he didn't answer their questions.

Exercise 3: Reflexive Pronouns

In the following sentences, identify the incorrect reflexive pronoun and rewrite the sentence using the correct pronoun.

1. The cat cleaned itself.
2. My sister and I went to the store.
3. The children made the cake themselves.

Chapter Three
Sentence Fragments And Run-on Sentences

Sentence fragments and run-on sentences are two common types of errors in writing that can cause confusion and detract from the clarity of a piece of writing. Understanding the differences between these two errors is essential to becoming a skilled writer. In this article, we will explore the definitions of sentence fragments and run-on sentences, their common causes, and some strategies for identifying and correcting them.

Sentence Fragments

A sentence fragment is an incomplete sentence that does not express a complete thought. A sentence fragment may be missing a subject, a verb, or a complete thought.

Examples of sentence fragments include:

1. Walking down the street.
2. Because he was tired and hungry.
3. While the sun was setting over the mountains.

In each of these examples, the sentence is incomplete and does not convey a complete thought. A sentence fragment can occur for several reasons, including:

A. **Missing subject or verb**: Sometimes, a sentence fragment is created when a subject or verb is missing. For example, "Walking down the street" is a fragment because it is missing a subject and a verb.

B. **Dependent clauses**: A dependent clause is a group of words that contains a subject and a verb but cannot stand alone as a sentence. For example, "Because he was tired and hungry" is a dependent clause and cannot stand alone as a sentence.

C. **Phrases**: A phrase is a group of words that does not contain a subject and a verb. For example, "While the sun was setting over the mountains" is a phrase and cannot stand alone as a sentence.

To correct a sentence fragment, you can:

i. **Add a subject or verb**: For example, "Walking down the street, I saw a beautiful sunset."
ii. **Combine with another sentence:** For example, "Because he was tired and hungry, he decided to stop at a restaurant."
iii. **Add a subject or verb to a phrase:** For example, "While the sun was setting over the mountains, I felt a sense of peace."

Run-On Sentences

A run-on sentence is a sentence that contains two or more independent clauses that are not properly connected. An independent clause is a group of words that contains a subject and a verb and can stand alone as a sentence. Examples of run-on sentences include:

1. I went to the store I bought some milk.
2. She was tired she went to bed early.
3. The movie was boring I fell asleep halfway through.

In each of these examples, the independent clauses are not properly connected and should be separated into two separate sentences. Run-on sentences can occur for several reasons, including:

A. **Lack of punctuation:** Sometimes, a run-on sentence occurs when two independent clauses are not separated by a period, semicolon, or other punctuation mark.

B. **Incorrect conjunction use**: A run-on sentence can occur when two independent clauses are connected by a conjunction that is not used correctly. For example, "She was tired but she went to bed early" is a correctly punctuated sentence, whereas "She was tired she went to bed early" is a run-on sentence

To correct a run-on sentence, you can:

i. **Separate into two sentences**: For example, "I went to the store. I bought some milk."
ii. **Use a comma and a coordinating conjunction**: For example, "She was tired, so she went to bed early."
iii. **Use a semicolon**: For example, "The movie was boring; I fell asleep halfway through."

Common Mistakes And How To Avoid Them

One of the most important aspects of good writing is clear and effective communication. However, many writers struggle with sentence fragments and run-on sentences, which can make their writing unclear and difficult to understand. In this article, we will explore these common mistakes and how to avoid them.

How to Avoid Sentence Fragments

1. **Check for subjects and verbs:** Make sure that every sentence has a subject and a verb. The subject is the person, place, or thing that performs the action, and the verb is the action itself.
2. **Avoid starting a sentence with a conjunction**: Conjunctions such as "and," "but," and "or"

are used to join two clauses together, but they should not be used to start a sentence on their own.

3. **Combine fragments with other sentences:** If you have a sentence fragment, try to combine it with another sentence to create a complete thought.

4. **Use punctuation correctly:** Make sure to use commas, semicolons, and other punctuation marks correctly to join clauses and create complete sentences.

How to Avoid Run-On Sentences

1. **Use proper punctuation:** Use a comma and a coordinating conjunction (and, but, or, nor, for, yet, so) to join two independent clauses.
2. **Use a semicolon:** Use a semicolon to join two independent clauses without a coordinating conjunction.
3. **Use a period**: Use a period to separate two independent clauses into two separate sentences.
4. **Use subordinate clauses:** Use subordinate clauses to connect two ideas and create a more complex sentence structure.

Practice Exercises

Read the following sentences carefully and determine whether they are sentence fragments, run-on sentences, or complete sentences. Then, rewrite any fragments and run-ons as complete sentences.
1. Walking through the park on a sunny day.
2. She didn't want to go to the party, she was tired.
3. Despite her best efforts, she couldn't finish the project on time. Which was disappointing.
4. He took his dog for a walk, he also stopped by the store to buy some milk.
5. Running late for the meeting, she grabbed her coat and ran out the door.

Chapter Four
Misplaced And Dangling Modifiers

Misplaced and dangling modifiers are two common errors in English grammar. Both types of modifiers are used to add more information to a sentence, but when they are misplaced or dangling, they can create confusion or change the intended meaning of the sentence. In this detailed page, we will explore the definitions of misplaced and dangling modifiers, examples of each, and how to correct them.

Misplaced Modifiers:

A misplaced modifier is a word or phrase that is placed in the wrong part of a sentence, which can create ambiguity or confusion. This can happen when the modifier is separated from the word or phrase it is meant to modify, or when it is placed next to the wrong word or phrase.

Example 1:

Misplaced: "Running down the street, the car hit the lamp post."

Corrected: "The car hit the lamp post while running down the street."

Explanation: In the original sentence, the modifier "running down the street" is placed before the subject "the car," which creates confusion about who or what was running down the street. The corrected sentence moves the modifier to the end of the sentence, making it clear that the car was the one running down the street.

Example *2*:

Misplaced: "I only eat vegetables for dinner."

Corrected: "For dinner, I only eat vegetables."

Explanation: In this sentence, the modifier "only" is misplaced because it is placed next to the verb "eat," which makes it unclear what the speaker is emphasizing. The corrected sentence moves the modifier to the beginning of the sentence, clarifying that the speaker only eats vegetables for dinner.

Dangling Modifiers:

A dangling modifier is a word or phrase that modifies a word or phrase that is not even in the sentence. This creates confusion or makes the sentence illogical because the modifier is not properly attached to the intended subject.

Example 1:

Dangling:"After studying for hours, the test was aced."

Corrected: "After studying for hours, she aced the test."

Explanation:In the original sentence, the modifier "after studying for hours" is dangling because it is not attached to any subject in the sentence. The corrected sentence adds the subject "she," making it clear who studied and aced the test.

Example 2:

Dangling:"To find the lost keys, the house was searched."

Corrected: "To find the lost keys, she searched the house."

Explanation:In this sentence, the modifier "to find the lost keys" is dangling because it is not attached to any subject in the sentence. The corrected sentence adds the subject "she," making it clear who searched the house to find the lost keys.

How to Correct Misplaced and Dangling Modifiers:

- ☐ To correct misplaced modifiers, you should place the modifier as close as possible to the word or phrase it is meant to modify. You may need to rearrange the sentence to do this.

- ☐ To correct dangling modifiers, you should add the subject that the modifier is intended to modify. This may involve adding a new subject or rephrasing the sentence entirely.

Misplaced and dangling modifiers can create confusion and alter the intended meaning of a sentence. By understanding the definitions of these modifiers and how to correct them, you can improve your writing and communication skills.

Practice Exercises

Exercise 1:

Misplaced Modifiers: *Rewrite the following sentences to correct the misplaced modifiers*

1. While driving to work, the sun rose over the horizon.
2. The baby was crawling on the floor in a diaper made of cotton.
3. She served sandwiches to the children on paper plates with mustard.
4. He saw a man with a telescope walking in the park.
5. After studying for hours, the exam was finally over.

Exercise 2:

<u>Dangling Modifiers:</u> *Rewrite the following sentences to correct the dangling modifiers:*

1. After running for hours, the mountain top was finally reached.
2. Not knowing the answer, the teacher had to help me with the question.
3. Walking down the street, the trees were beautiful in the fall.
4. Having been raised on a farm, the city was overwhelming to her.
5. To learn English quickly, the book was recommended by the teacher.

Chapter Five
Comma Usage

Comma usage is an important aspect of grammar that helps to clarify meaning, separate ideas, and create structure in writing. Correct comma usage can significantly improve the readability and comprehension of a text. In this detailed page, we will explore the different rules of comma usage, including when to use commas, where to place them, and common mistakes to avoid.

1. To separate items in a list: Commas are commonly used to separate items in a list. For example, in the sentence "I need to buy apples, oranges, and bananas," commas are used to separate the three items in the list. The final comma before the conjunction "and" is known as the Oxford comma and is optional in some writing styles.

2. To separate two independent clauses: When two independent clauses are joined by a coordinating conjunction (and, but, or, nor, for, yet, so), a comma should be used before the conjunction. For example, in the sentence "I am going to the store, and I need to buy some milk," a comma is used to separate the two independent clauses.

3. To separate introductory phrases or clauses: A comma is used to separate an introductory phrase or clause from the main clause of a sentence. For example, in the sentence "After finishing my homework, I went for a walk," the comma separates the introductory phrase "After finishing my homework" from the main clause "I went for a walk."

4. To set off non-essential information: Commas can be used to set off non-essential information in a sentence, such as appositives, interrupters, or non-essential clauses. For example, in the sentence "My friend, who lives in New York, is coming to visit," the comma sets off the non-essential clause "who lives in New York."

5. To separate adjectives: Commas are used to separate two or more adjectives that describe the same noun. For example, in the sentence "She has beautiful, long hair," the comma separates the two adjectives "beautiful" and "long."

6. To clarify meaning: Commas can be used to clarify meaning in a sentence. For example, in the sentence "I love cooking my family and my pets," the lack of a

comma after "cooking" suggests that the speaker enjoys cooking their family and pets. To clarify that they mean to cook for their family and for their pets, a comma should be inserted after "cooking."

Mistakes to avoid:

1. Overusing commas: While commas are useful, overusing them can lead to choppy sentences and confusion. Be sure to use commas only when necessary.

2. Not using commas where they are needed: Leaving out necessary commas can also cause confusion and ambiguity. Be sure to follow the rules of comma usage to ensure clarity in your writing.

3. Placing commas incorrectly: Misplaced commas can also change the meaning of a sentence. Be sure to place commas in the correct position according to the rules of comma usage.

Comma Usage is an important aspect of grammar that helps to create structure and clarity in writing. By following the rules of comma usage and avoiding common mistakes, you can improve the readability and comprehension of your writing

Most Common Mistakes And How To Avoid Them

Commas are one of the most commonly used punctuation marks in the English language. However, they can also be one of the most confusing punctuation marks, as many people struggle with knowing when to use them and when to avoid them. In this article, we will discuss some of the most common mistakes people make when using commas and how to avoid them.

1. **Using commas to separate complete sentences**: One of the most common mistakes people make when using commas is using them to separate two complete sentences. This is known as a comma splice, and it is considered incorrect grammar. To avoid this mistake, you can use a conjunction (such as "and" or "but") or a semicolon to join the two sentences together, or you can separate them into two separate sentences.

Example of comma splice: I went to the store, I bought some milk.

Corrected version: I went to the store and bought some milk. OR I went to the store; I bought some milk. OR I went to the store. I bought some milk.

2. **Using commas to separate two adjectives:** Another common mistake people make is using a comma to separate two adjectives that are describing the same noun. When two adjectives are used together to describe a noun, they should be separated by "and" or no punctuation at all.

Example: She has long, brown hair.

Corrected version: She has long brown hair.

3. **Using commas in compound nouns**: A compound noun is a noun that is made up of two or more words. When a compound noun is used, it should not be separated by commas.

Example of incorrect use: The fire, truck arrived at the scene.

Corrected version: The fire truck arrived at the scene.

4. **Using commas with introductory phrases or clauses:** When an introductory phrase or clause is used, it should be followed by a comma to separate it from the rest of the sentence.

Example: In the morning, I like to drink coffee.

Corrected version: In the morning, I like to drink coffee.

5. **Using commas in lists:** When listing three or more items, a comma should be used to separate each item.

Example: My favorite colors are red, blue, and green.

Corrected version: My favorite colors are red, blue and green.

6. **Not using commas to set off nonessential information**: Nonessential information is information that can be removed from a sentence without changing the meaning of the sentence. When nonessential information is used, it should be set off by commas.

Example of incorrect use: John who is my friend, is coming over for dinner.

Corrected version: John, who is my friend, is coming over for dinner.

7. **Not using commas to set off direct address:** When addressing someone directly, their name or title should be set off by commas.

Example of incorrect use: How are you Susan?

Corrected version: How are you, Susan?

By being aware of these common mistakes, you can avoid them and use commas correctly in your writing. Remember, using proper grammar and punctuation can help make your writing more clear and effective.

Practice Exercises

Exercise 1:

Add or remove commas where necessary in the following sentences.

1. My favorite foods are pizza hamburgers and ice cream.
2. After I finished my homework I went to bed.
3. The concert was canceled however we still had a great time in the city.
4. I need to buy milk bread and eggs at the store.
5. Although she was tired she kept working.

Exercise 2:

Identify whether there is comma errors placed in the following sentences and correct them.

1. She cooked the food, and I cleaned the dishes.
2. The dog, which was barking loudly, ran after the mailman.
3. My favorite colors are red, green, blue and yellow.
4. In the morning I like to have coffee, toast and orange juice.
5. During the summer I like to go to the beach, swim and read books.

Exercise 3:

Rewrite the following sentences to avoid comma splices.

1. I woke up late, I missed the bus.
2. She loves to read, she also enjoys playing tennis.
3. The sun was setting, the sky was a beautiful shade of pink and orange.
4. We studied all night for the exam, we still didn't do well.
5. He's very talented, he can play the guitar, piano, and drums

Chapter Six
Apostrophe Usage

The apostrophe is a small punctuation mark that is often misunderstood and misused in written English. It is used to indicate possession, contraction, and occasionally, plurals. Proper use of the apostrophe can greatly improve the clarity and effectiveness of your writing, while incorrect use can result in confusion and errors. In this guide, we will explore the rules for apostrophe usage and provide examples to help you master this important punctuation mark.

Possessive Apostrophe:

One of the most common uses of the apostrophe is to indicate possession.

The general rule is that an apostrophe and an "s" are added to the end of a singular noun to indicate ownership, and the apostrophe alone is added to the end of a plural noun to indicate ownership.

For example:

1. The boy's ball (the ball belonging to the boy)
2. The dogs' toys (the toys belonging to the dogs)

If the plural form of the noun does not end in "s", an apostrophe and "s" are added to indicate ownership.

For example:

1. The children's books (the books belonging to the children)
2. The women's shoes (the shoes belonging to the women)

It's important to note that the apostrophe is not used to indicate the plural of a noun, unless the noun is an abbreviation or acronym. In these cases, an apostrophe and an "s" are added to the end of the noun to indicate the plural.

For example:

1. The CEO's of the company (referring to multiple CEOs)
2. The DVD's in the collection (referring to multiple DVDs)

Contractions:

Another common use of the apostrophe is to create contractions. Contractions are two words that are combined and shortened by replacing one or more letters with an apostrophe.

For example:

1. It is -> It's
2. Do not -> Don't
3. I will -> I'll

Contractions are informal and should generally be avoided in formal writing. However, they can be used to create a conversational tone or to mimic spoken language in dialogue or first-person writing.

Plurals:

While the apostrophe is not typically used to indicate plurals, there are a few exceptions. The apostrophe is used to indicate the plural of lowercase letters, numbers, and some abbreviations.

For example:

1. Mind your p's and q's (referring to the letters "p" and "q")
2. I got all A's on my report card (referring to the letter "A")
3. The 1990's were a time of change (referring to the decade of the 1990s)

It's important to note that the apostrophe is not used to indicate the plural of proper nouns, such as names or titles

For example:

1. The Johnsons (referring to a family with the last name Johnson)
2. The Smiths (referring to a family with the last name Smith)
3. The Kennedys (referring to the famous political family)

Common Mistakes And How To Avoid Them

Apostrophes are a frequently used punctuation mark in the English language. They can be used to indicate possession or to indicate the omission of letters in contractions. However, apostrophes are also a common source of errors in writing. In this article, we will discuss some common mistakes in apostrophe usage and how to avoid them.

1. Confusing its and it's:

One of the most common apostrophe errors is the confusion between "its" and "it's."

"It's" is a contraction of "it is" or "it has," while "its" is a possessive pronoun. The apostrophe is not used in the possessive form of "its."

Correct usage:

1. It's a beautiful day today.
2. The dog wagged its tail.

2. Using apostrophes with plural nouns:

Apostrophes are not used to make a noun plural. They are only used to indicate possession or to form contractions. Using apostrophes with plural nouns is a common mistake.

Incorrect usage*: I have three dog's.

Correct usage:I have three dogs.

3. Confusing plurals and possessives:

Another common mistake is confusing plurals and possessives. The apostrophe is used to indicate possession, but not for plural nouns that do not possess something.

Correct usage:

1. The children's toys were scattered on the floor.
2. The dogs ran through the fields.

Incorrect usage:

1. The dog's played in the park.
2. The childrens' toys were scattered on the floor

4. Using apostrophes with possessive pronouns:

Possessive pronouns, such as "yours," "theirs," and "ours," already indicate possession and do not require an apostrophe.

Correct usage:

1. The book is yours.
2. That is theirs to keep

Incorrect usage:

1. That book is your's.
2. That is their's to keep

5. Using apostrophes with acronyms and numbers:

Apostrophes are not used to form plurals with acronyms and numbers.

Correct usage: I got all A's on my report card.

Incorrect usage: I got all As on my report card.

Apostrophes are a useful punctuation mark, but they can be misused. By understanding the common mistakes in apostrophe usage and how to avoid them, you can improve your writing and communicate more effectively. Remember to only use apostrophes to indicate possession or to form contractions, and not for plural nouns or possessive pronouns.

Practice Exercises

Exercise 1:

Identify the incorrect use of apostrophes in the following sentences and correct them.

1. The boys' room was messy.
2. Its a great day for a picnic.
3. My parents' house is on the corner.
4. The cat's food bowl is empty.
5. Im going to the movies tonight.

Exercise 2:

Rewrite the following sentences without using any contractions.

1. It's time to go to the store.
2. You're not allowed to smoke in here.
3. He's been working on that project for weeks.
4. She's going to meet us at the park.
5. We're going to have a party next weekend.

Exercise 3:

Complete the following sentences by using the correct form of the apostrophe.

1. The _________ car door was dented.
2. _________ plans for the weekend include going to the beach.
3. _________ dog barked at the mailman.
4. _________ favorite color is blue.
5. The _________ office is closed on Sundays.

<u>Exercise 4:</u>

Identify the mistake in the following sentence and correct it.

1. The teacher's assigned the students to read "To Kill a Mockingbird."

2. My parents' went on vacation to Hawaii.

3. Its a good thing we brought umbrellas, because it rained all day.

4. Im sorry, but I cant come to the party tonight.

5. The dogs tail wagged happily as it greeted its owner

<u>Exercise 4:</u>

Chapter Seven
Confusing Words

Confusing words are words that have similar spellings or pronunciations but different meanings. They are a common source of errors in writing and communication, and can lead to confusion and misunderstandings. In this article, we will discuss some of the most common confusing words in English, their definitions, and how to use them correctly.

1. Affect and Effect: These two words are often used interchangeably, but they have distinct meanings. Affect is a verb that means to influence or have an impact on something. Effect is a noun that means the result or consequence of an action.

   Example: The new policy will affect our sales next quarter. The effect of the new policy on our sales is yet to be determined.

2. Accept and Except: Accept is a verb that means to receive or agree to something. Except is a preposition that means excluding or with the exception of.

   Example: I will accept the job offer, except for the salary.

3. Principle and Principal: Principle is a noun that means a fundamental truth or belief. Principal is a noun that means the head of a school or an amount of money lent or invested.

   Example: The principal of the school is a firm believer in the principle of equality.

4. Complement and Compliment: Complement is a noun that means something that completes or enhances something else. Compliment is a noun that means an expression of praise or admiration.

   Example: The red shoes complement her blue dress. She received a compliment on her new hairstyle.

5. Stationary and Stationery: Stationary is an adjective that means not moving or fixed in place. Stationery is a noun that refers to writing materials.

   Example: The car was stationary at the red light. She bought some new stationery for her desk.

6. Their, There and They're: These three words are often confused in writing. Their is

a possessive pronoun that shows ownership. There is an adverb that refers to a place or location. They're is a contraction of they are.

Example: Their dog is barking over there. They're going to the park later.

7. Its and It's: Its is a possessive pronoun that shows ownership. It's is a contraction of it is.

   Example: The company increased its revenue this year. It's raining outside.

8. Than and Then: Than is a conjunction used in comparisons. Then is an adverb that refers to a point in time or a sequence of events.

   Example: She is taller than her sister. We went to the store, and then we went to the park.

9. Your and You're: Your is a possessive pronoun that shows ownership. You're is a contraction of you are.

   Example: Your phone is ringing. You're going to be late for the meeting.

10. Advise and Advice: Advise is a verb that means to give counsel or advice. Advice is a noun that refers to recommendations or guidance.

    Example: I advise you to speak with a financial advisor for advice on investing.

Confusing words can be a stumbling block for many writers and communicators. It is important to be aware of their differences and use them correctly to avoid misunderstandings and errors. Always take the time to double-check your work and consult a dictionary or writing resource when in doubt.

Practice Exercises

Exercise 1: On Common Mistakes

Read the following sentences and identify the common mistakes. Then, rewrite the sentences correctly.

1. *I seen that movie last night.*
2. *Him and me went to the store.*
3. *They was late for the meeting.*
4. *The book is laying on the table.*
5. *She don't like coffee.*

Exercise 2: Avoiding Confusing Words

Fill in the blanks with the correct word from the pair of confusing words provided.

1. *She is going to ____________ (lie, lay) down for a nap.*

2. *The team ____________ (lose, loose) the game by one point.*

3. *I need to ____________ (accept, except) this invitation before it expires.*

4. *The cat ____________ (licked, liked) its paws after eating.*

5. *He ____________ (complimented, complemented) her outfit at the party.*

Chapter Eight
Capitalization and Punctuation

Capitalization and punctuation are important aspects of written communication that help to convey meaning and clarity to the reader. Both of these elements play a crucial role in the construction and interpretation of sentences and paragraphs, and are essential tools for effective writing.

Capitalization:

Capitalization refers to the use of capital letters in writing. Capital letters are used to indicate the beginning of a sentence or the start of a proper noun, such as the name of a person, place, or organization. In addition, capital letters are often used for titles of books, movies, and other works of art.

It is important to note that not all words need to be capitalized. For example, common nouns like "car," "tree," and "house" do not require capitalization, unless they are used as part of a proper noun, such as "Ford car," "Oak tree," or "White House."

When it comes to capitalization in titles of works, there are specific rules that vary depending on the style guide being followed. Generally, the first word and all major words in a title should be capitalized, while minor words such as "a," "an," "the," "and," and "of" are not capitalized, unless they are the first or last word in the title.

Punctuation:

Punctuation refers to the use of symbols such as periods, commas, question marks, and exclamation points to separate and clarify the meaning of words and phrases in a sentence.

One of the most important punctuation marks is the period, which is used to indicate the end of a sentence. Commas are used to separate items in a list or to separate clauses in a sentence. Question marks are used to indicate a question, while exclamation points are used to indicate strong emotion or emphasis.

Other important punctuation marks include the colon and semicolon, which are used to separate clauses or to indicate a pause in the flow of a sentence. Quotation marks are used to indicate dialogue or to indicate the use of a specific word or phrase.

It is important to use punctuation marks correctly in order to avoid confusion or ambiguity in your writing. Incorrect use of punctuation can change the meaning of a sentence or make it difficult to understand.

Capitalization and punctuation are important tools for effective written communication. Correct use of these elements can help to convey meaning and clarity, while incorrect use can lead to confusion or misinterpretation. It is important to understand the rules and guidelines for capitalization and punctuation in order to produce clear and effective writing.

Common Mistakes And How To Avoid Them

Capitalization and punctuation are crucial elements of written communication. They help convey meaning, clarify relationships between words, and create a smooth flow of information. However, many people struggle with these aspects of writing and make common mistakes that can undermine the effectiveness of their writing. In this article, we will discuss some of the most common capitalization and punctuation errors and provide tips on how to avoid them.

Capitalization Errors:

1. Not Capitalizing Proper Nouns: Proper nouns refer to specific people, places, or things, and they should always be capitalized. For example, the names of cities, countries, people, and brands should all be capitalized. For instance, "London" and "Apple" are proper nouns that should always be capitalized.

2. Capitalizing Common Nouns: Unlike proper nouns, common nouns such as "dog," "car," or "house" are not capitalized unless they are at the beginning of a sentence or part of a title. For example, in the sentence "I have a red car," only "car" should be in lowercase.

3. Capitalizing Every Word in a Sentence: This mistake often happens in titles or headings. However, it's incorrect to capitalize every word in a sentence except for prepositions, conjunctions, and articles. For example, "The Boy Who Lived" is correct, while "The Boy Who Lived and Played with His Cat" is incorrect.

4. Incorrect Use of Capital Letters in Acronyms: Acronyms are words formed by the

first letters of several words. It's common to capitalize every letter in an acronym, but it's not always necessary. For instance, the acronym "NASA" should always be capitalized, but "AIDS" and "UNICEF" are in all caps because they are pronounced like regular words.

Punctuation Errors:

1. <u>Not Using Commas Correctly</u>: Commas are used to separate clauses, items in a list, and to set off introductory phrases or clauses. Using commas incorrectly can lead to confusion and ambiguity in a sentence. For example, "I love cooking my family and my dog" is incorrect because it's unclear whether the speaker loves cooking for their family and dog or cooking their family and dog.

2. <u>Using Apostrophes Incorrectly</u>: Apostrophes are used to indicate possession or to form contractions. The most common mistake is using an apostrophe to make a word plural. For example, "I have two dog's" is incorrect, while "I have two dogs" is correct.

3. <u>Overusing Exclamation Points</u>: Exclamation points are used to express strong emotions or to emphasize a statement. However, using too many exclamation points can make the writing seem amateurish or overly dramatic.

4. <u>Not Using Hyphens Correctly</u>: Hyphens are used to link words together and to avoid ambiguity. For example, "re-paint" is hyphenated because it links two words together, while "repaint" without a hyphen is a different word that means to paint again.

How to Avoid These Mistakes:

1. Proofread Carefully: Always proofread your work before submitting or publishing it. Check for capitalization and punctuation errors, and make sure that your writing is clear and easy to understand.

2. Use Grammar and Spellcheck Tools: Use grammar and spellcheck tools to catch any errors that you might have missed.

3. Review Writing Guidelines: Consult writing guidelines for the specific type of writing you are doing. For example, if you're writing a scientific paper, consult the

guidelines from the journal you're submitting to.

4. <u>Practice</u>: Practice writing and identifying capitalization and punctuation errors. The more you practice, the more you'll improve.

Practice Exercises

Exercise 1:

a) *Rewrite the following sentence using correct capitalization:*

The president of the united states is joe biden.

b) *Correct the capitalization errors in the following sentence:*

1. jessica wants to study psychology at the university of michigan.
2. my favorite movies are the godfather, rocky, and pulp fiction.

Exercise 2:

(a) *Add the missing punctuation marks to the following sentence:*

i went to the store bought milk bread cheese and eggs.

(b) *Correct the punctuation errors in the following sentence:*

1. i woke up early but i was still late for my appointment.
2. sarah loves to read books, she has a huge collection of them.

Exercise 3:

a) *Identify and correct the errors in the following sentence:*

1. the restaurant was very good, the food was delicious and the service was fast.
2. john went to the mall to buy clothes, shoes, and a watch.
3. I want to learn spanish, french, and german because i love to travel.

Chapter Nine
Commonly Misspelled Words

Spelling is an essential skill in written communication. It is the act of writing words correctly and accurately, ensuring that they convey the intended message. However, many words in the English language are commonly misspelled. These words can cause confusion and misinterpretation of the message being conveyed. Therefore, it is important to be aware of these commonly misspelled words to ensure effective written communication. In this detailed page, we will discuss some of the most commonly misspelled words in the English language and provide tips on how to avoid misspelling them.

1. Accommodation: This word is often misspelled because of its double 'c' and double 'm'. To remember the correct spelling, try to break the word down into syllables: ac-com-mo-da-tion.

2. Definitely: Many people spell this word as "definately" or "defiantly". A useful tip to remember the correct spelling is to break the word down into syllables and remember that it ends in "itely."

3. Embarrass: This word is often misspelled because of the double 'r' and double 's'. To remember the correct spelling, try to break the word down into syllables: em-bar-rass.

4. Occurrence: This word is often misspelled because of the double 'c' and double 'r'. To remember the correct spelling, try to break the word down into syllables: oc-cur-rence.

5. Separate: This word is often misspelled as "seperate" because of the tendency to confuse the 'a' and 'e' in the word. A useful tip to remember the correct spelling is to think of the word as having the word "a rat" in the middle of it.

6. Receive: This word is often misspelled because of the 'i' and 'e' in the middle of the word. A useful tip to remember the correct spelling is to think of the phrase "I before E, except after C."

7. <u>Privilege</u>: This word is often misspelled because of the double 'i' and double 'e'. To remember the correct spelling, try to break the word down into syllables: priv-i-lege.

8. <u>Maintenance</u>: This word is often misspelled because of the 'a' and 'e' in the middle of the word. A useful tip to remember the correct spelling is to think of the phrase "main-ten-ance".

9. <u>Parallel</u>: This word is often misspelled because of the double 'l' at the end of the word. A useful tip to remember the correct spelling is to think of the word as having two parallel lines.

10. <u>A lot:</u> This phrase is often misspelled as "alot" because it is often used as one word. However, it is important to remember that "a lot" is two words.

How To Avoid Commonly Misspelled Words

☐ <u>Use a Spell Checker</u>: One of the easiest ways to avoid spelling mistakes is to use a spell checker. Most word processors and writing software come with built-in spell checkers that will highlight misspelled words and suggest corrections. While spell checkers are not foolproof and can miss some errors, they are a useful tool to catch obvious mistakes.

☐ <u>Double-Check Homophones</u>: Homophones are words that sound the same but have different spellings and meanings. Examples include "their" and "there," "its" and "it's," and "your" and "you're." These words can be easy to confuse, so it's essential to double-check that you're using the correct spelling and meaning for the context.

☐ <u>Learn Spelling Rules</u>: English has many spelling rules that can help you understand why words are spelled the way they are. For example, the "i before e except after c" rule states that in most cases, "i" comes before "e" in a word, except after "c." Learning these rules can help you to spell words correctly even if you've never seen them before.

☐ <u>Make a List of Problem Words</u>: If you find that you consistently misspell certain words, make a list of these words and keep it handy. You can refer to this list when you're writing to ensure that you're spelling these words correctly.

☐ <u>Read, Read, Read</u>: Reading is an excellent way to improve your spelling skills. When you read, you're exposed to a wide variety of words, and you'll begin to recognize correct spellings more easily. Additionally, reading can help you to understand how words are used in context, which can be helpful when you're trying to determine the correct spelling of a word.

☐ <u>Practice, Practice, Practice</u>: Like any skill, spelling takes practice. Make an effort to practice your spelling regularly, whether that's by writing in a journal, sending emails to friends, or taking spelling quizzes online. The more you practice, the more confident you'll become in your spelling abilities.

Practice Exercises

Here are some special events you should involve yourself into, in order to improve your Spelling Ability:

1. <u>Spelling Bee</u>: Divide the class into teams and hold a spelling bee using a list of commonly misspelled words. Each team can take turns choosing a word from the list and attempting to spell it correctly. This exercise can be made more challenging by using words with homophones or words that have similar spellings.

2. <u>Word Scramble</u>: Create a list of commonly misspelled words and scramble the letters. Have the students unscramble the words and write the correct spelling next to each scrambled word.

3. <u>Fill in the Blanks</u>: Create a worksheet with sentences that contain commonly misspelled words. Leave the misspelled words blank and have the students fill in the correct spelling.

4. <u>Crossword Puzzle</u>: Create a crossword puzzle using commonly misspelled words as the clues. The students can use a dictionary to look up the correct spelling of each word before filling in the crossword.

5. <u>Dictation Exercise</u>: Read a passage that contains commonly misspelled

words aloud to the class. Have the students write down each word as they hear it, paying close attention to spelling. After the exercise, go over the correct spellings as a class.

Conclusion

In conclusion, "Master Your Writing: A Comprehensive Guide to Correcting Common

Grammar Mistakes" is an exceptional guidebook that will help you improve your writing skills significantly. The book is designed to help writers of all levels overcome common grammar mistakes, enhance their writing style, and polish their final product.

With its clear and concise explanations, comprehensive examples, and practical exercises, "Master Your Writing" is an invaluable resource for anyone looking to perfect their writing skills. From grammar basics to advanced techniques, this book covers everything a writer needs to know to produce high-quality writing that is free of errors.

Moreover, the book is structured in a way that makes it easy to navigate and understand, with each chapter focusing on a specific aspect of grammar and style. The author's writing style is engaging and accessible, making it easy for readers to follow along and retain the information presented.

Whether you are a student, professional writer, or just someone who wants to improve their writing skills, "Master Your Writing" is the perfect resource for you. By mastering the grammar rules and techniques outlined in this book, you will be able to communicate your ideas clearly, effectively, and with confidence.

In summary, "Master Your Writing: A Comprehensive Guide to Correcting Common Grammar Mistakes" is a must-read for anyone who wants to improve their writing skills. The book is well-organized, easy to read, and packed with practical tips and exercises that will help you take your writing to the next level. If you are serious about becoming a better writer, this book is the perfect place to start.

Final Tips And Advice For Improving Grammar Skills

Improving grammar skills can be a daunting task, but it is an essential skill that can help you communicate effectively in both written and spoken forms. While there is no single formula for improving grammar skills, there are several tips and strategies you can use to enhance your writing and speaking abilities. Here are some final tips and advice for improving your grammar skills.

Read regularly

Reading is an effective way to improve your grammar skills. Reading helps you to familiarize yourself with sentence structures, grammar rules, and common vocabulary. By reading regularly, you can absorb different writing styles, techniques, and sentence structures, which can help you become a better writer and speaker.

Practice writing

Writing is an essential skill for improving grammar. Practice writing every day, whether it is a journal entry, an email, or a short story. By writing regularly, you can identify your grammar weaknesses, such as spelling, punctuation, and sentence structure, and work on improving them.

Use grammar apps and tools

There are several grammar apps and tools available online that can help you improve your grammar skills. These apps and tools can identify your grammar errors and suggest corrections. Some popular grammar apps include Grammarly, Hemingway, and ProWritingAid.

Join a writing group or workshop

Joining a writing group or workshop is an excellent way to improve your grammar skills. These groups provide a supportive environment where you can receive feedback on your writing and learn from other writers. Writing groups and workshops can help you identify your weaknesses and strengths and give you constructive feedback on how to improve your grammar skills.

Take a grammar course

Taking a grammar course is an effective way to improve your grammar skills. There are several online courses and classes available that can help you learn grammar rules and practice applying them. Some popular online grammar courses include The

Great Courses Plus, Coursera, and Udemy.

<u>Keep it simple</u>

One of the most important rules of grammar is to keep it simple. Use simple, clear language that is easy to understand. Avoid using complicated sentences, jargon, or technical terms that can confuse your readers or listeners. Simplifying your language can help you communicate your message effectively.

Improving your grammar skills takes time, patience, and practice. By following these tips and strategies, you can enhance your writing and speaking abilities and become a better communicator. Remember to read regularly, practice writing, use grammar apps and tools, join a writing group or workshop, take a grammar course, and keep it simple. With dedication and hard work, you can master grammar and become an excellent writer and speaker.